Secret Cities

by Mike Corbishley

illustrated by Roger Wade Walker
and with photographs

Lodestar Books

E. P. Dutton   New York

Originally published in Great Britain 1989 by
Hamish Hamilton Children's Books

First published in the United States 1989 by
E. P. Dutton, New York, New York,
a division of NAL Penguin Inc.

Copyright © in this format Belitha Press Ltd 1989
Designer: Gillian Riley
Editor: Felicity Trotman
Printed in Hong Kong by Imago Publishing
First Edition COBE 10 9 8 7 6 5 4 3 2 1

Conceived, designed and produced by
Belitha Press Ltd
31 Newington Green, London N16 9PU

Library of Congress Cataloging-in-Publication Data

Corbishley, Mike.
  Secret Cities.
  Includes index.
  Summary: Describes cities, covering a time
span of 8000 years, which have been excavated or
restored, and speculates on the civilization of
each as evidenced by what remains.
  1. Historic buildings – Juvenile literature.
2. Cities and towns, Ruined, extinct, etc. –
Juvenile literature. 3. Cities and towns,
Ancient – Juvenile literature. 4. Civilization,
Ancient – Juvenile literature. [1. Cities and
towns, Ancient. 2. Civilization, Ancient.]
  I. Walker, Roger Wade, ill. II. Title.
  CC135.C64 1989 930 88-31101
  ISBN 0-525-67275-3

The publishers wish to thank the following for permission
to reproduce copyright material:

The Ancient Art and Architecture Collection, pp 43,
44 *both* (photographs by B. Norman)
Aspect Picture Library, p 30
Martii Kainulainen, Colorific! p 33
Robert Harding Picture Library, pp 7, 14, 20, 29 *both*, 31,
34 *top right*, 37 *top left*, 38, 40 *top right*
The British Museum, p 6 (kindly lent by the Folio Society)
The Peabody Museum, Harvard University, p 37 *bottom*

right, photographed by Hillel Burger
The State Archeological Museum, Warsaw, pp 11 *top*,
bottom right
Pedicini snc, p 27
Picturepoint, pp 18, 21, 25, 28, 45
Andrzej Ring, pp 10 *both*, 11 *bottom left*
South American Pictures, pp 39, 40 *centre left*
Xinhua News Agency, pp 32, 34 *bottom left*, 35 *both*
York Archaeological Trust Picture Library, pp 12, 13 *all*
Map and diagrams by Gillian Riley
Artwork on pp 26 and 27 courtesy of Chris Molan

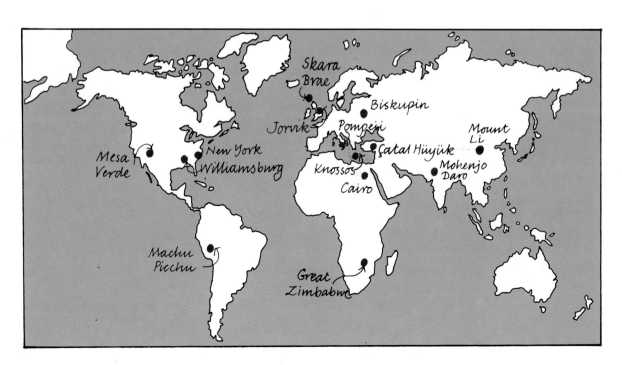

Contents

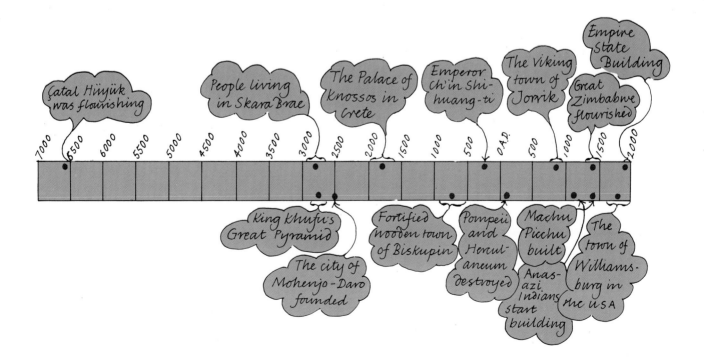

This book is about different types of buildings put up by people in the past. You will read about, and see, buildings from 8,000 years ago to more modern times—buildings for living, working, and worshiping. There is even a huge Chinese city of the dead for you to discover on page 32.

These buried buildings are from many parts of the world, from Peru to Pakistan. Each place has been discovered, often in a very exciting way—exciting for the archeologists who look for clues to help them understand the way people lived in the past. As you read this book, become an archeological detective—look for the clues and try to work out what they mean. To help you we are going to begin with something familiar....

Look carefully at the drawing opposite of one type of modern house. You'll recognize the front yard with its fence and gate, the car under its shelter and the house itself. Part of the roof has been left off so that you can see inside. You can begin right away being a detective by considering what the building is used for. Look for the clues. What tells you it's a house and not a factory or a church? If it's used to live in, how many people live here?

Now in the drawing on the right you have to begin to be an archeological detective. This house has been abandoned, or left. The roof has gone and bits of the building are falling apart. Someone has taken all the objects from the house. However, there are still quite a few clues left for you.

After many years the building might look like this. All the wooden parts (like the roof, doors, window frames, and fence) have rotted away. Some of the walls have fallen down, or perhaps been removed for building elsewhere. As an archeological detective you would have to work harder to figure out what happened here in the past. Careful observation and recording are vital now.

Many, many years later, the house has practically disappeared. Humps and bumps in the field reveal where the walls once stood. As an archeological detective you recognize clues like this. To discover more about the building and the people who lived there you would have to excavate. From this excavation you might discover the plan, or shape, of the house. If you were lucky you might find where the yard fence posts stood in the ground. You might also find evidence in the form of objects lost or thrown away.

What would the evidence of these objects tell you about the people who once lived here?

1 Skara Brae A Village of Farmers

The wind blew off the cold Atlantic Ocean far, far in the north of Scotland. The seas were whipped up into a frenzy and lashed the little Bay of Skaill on the island of Orkney. Suddenly the ferocious winds tore at the grass on top of the sand dune the local people called Skara Brae. As the grass was uprooted and bowled across the heather, the unprotected sand quickly blew away.

Under the lumpy sand dune the morning after that storm in the winter of 1850, a whole village was revealed. The landowner, William Watt, began to investigate, and gradually uncovered the houses of the village. Now, more than one hundred years later, after more recent excavations, the whole site is revealed.

It's a small village of about nine houses and a village workshop. All the houses are joined together. They are either built alongside one another or connected by narrow passageways. Look into the house pictured above. It's neatly laid out with a fireplace in the middle for cooking and warmth. Can you see the stone furniture around the walls? Look for the dresser

with its shelves, the box bed filled with soft heather, the cupboards tucked away in the walls and the watertight containers sunk into the floor to hold bait for fishing.

Garbage from these houses was dumped in heaps between buildings, around the outside, and on top of the roofs. Archeologists worked through this garbage and found plenty of bones, mostly of cattle and sheep but also of pigs, deer, and dogs. There were also bones of codfish, shells of crabs, limpets, and other shellfish. There were some bird bones (gannets were popular) and birds' eggs. Look at the picture and you will find grain (it's barley) being ground into flour. There are also ropes made from plaited heather, and wooden, bone, and flint tools as well as pots made of baked clay.

Today salt sea water laps the edge of this village. When it was first occupied, it was probably on the edge of a freshwater lagoon, near the sea.

The house walls and passageways were constructed of slabs of local stone. The passageways were roofed with stone but the houses had roofs of timber (driftwood from the sea), or whalebone, that were covered with turfs, heather, and garbage.

What can archeologists tell from this evidence? As the villagers had left behind grain and many bones of animals that were not wild (such as the sheep), they must have been farmers. There was also plenty of evidence of hunting (deer bones), fishing (fish bones, limpets for bait), and food gathering (shellfish). No evidence of metal tools was found. This all adds up to the conclusion that the village was occupied by some of the earliest farmers in Britain—in the period called the neolithic or New Stone Age. Radiocarbon dating has revealed that people were living at Skara Brae from about 3100 to about 2450 B.C. How did the village become deserted? Oddly enough, it's thought that it was abandoned because the sand constantly blew over the village. It became completely covered and hidden with a sand dune, to be discovered 4,300 years later.

Warfare and defense were on people's minds throughout Europe during the Iron Age. At Biskupin, 156 miles (250 kilometers) west of Warsaw in Poland, an extraordinary site was first unearthed in 1933—a town built entirely of wood: the defenses are wooden, the houses are wooden, even the streets are wooden! What's more, if you visit the site today you can actually wander along the streets or climb up onto the defenses because part of this town has been reconstructed.

This town, lived in between the eighth and the fifth centuries B.C., was built on an island in a lake, now called Biskupin, and was joined to the mainland by a causeway 130 yards (120 meters) long. Because the site became waterlogged, the timbers were well preserved, and archeologists have been able to work out an accurate picture of the town. A defensive wall, constructed like a timber box full of earth and clay, surrounds the entire town, which had only one strongly guarded entrance. Each family lived in one unit of the very long buildings that stretched the width of the town—a bit like row houses, or apartments all built at ground level.

FACT BOX

9,340 cubic yards (7,155 cubic meters) of timber were needed to build Biskupin.

If you walked around the entire wall you would have covered 1,368 feet (417 meters).

This is a reconstruction of one of the houses at Biskupin. Here is the main room with a hearth in the centre. Notice how the fire has to be built on a bed of large stones—this is for safety in a building made entirely of wood and thatch. At one end is the sleeping area. Animals were kept in the house as well and the upper story, reached by a ladder, was used to store animal feed, straw, and food.

The reconstructed site as visitors see it today. In some of the original houses lived families of craftspeople, specializing in weaving, metalworking, and bone carving.

Why was it so well planned, with families in almost identical houses? It could have been the grand design of some chief or leader, but there is no big house for such an important person. Perhaps the people of Biskupin decided on the layout of the town for themselves by voting, or through an elected council. What do you think?

The people were farmers, mainly of cattle, but they also bred pigs, sheep, and goats. They had dogs and horses, too. They grew a variety of crops, including wheat, barley, and vegetables. They added to their diet by fishing for pike, carp, and bream, and hunted wild animals like deer, boars, and hares.

These pictures show how precisely the town was laid out. The longest rows contain ten houses, and archeologists estimate that there were between 700 and 1,000 people living in more than 100 houses inside Biskupin.

Excavations at Biskupin were interrupted by the invasion of the Nazis during World War II. They destroyed all previous records and kept none during their two-month investigation of the site. After taking down the reconstructions of the buildings, they abandoned the site. Excavations began again in 1947, after the war.

3 Jorvik A Viking Town

FACT BOX

Jorvik was found under the street called Coppergate.

Coppergate comes from two Viking words, *kopr* (cup) and *gata* (street). Coppergate was the street of the wooden cup makers.

In York today you can visit the reconstructed Viking houses.

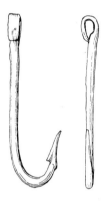

The iron fishhook was only one way to catch fish—people also used nets and traps. The people of Jorvik ate quantities of pickled herrings, and also salmon, eels, pike, perch, roach, plaice, and cod.

Leather working was an important industry in Jorvik. These shoes were only some of many products which included belts, gloves, and sword scabbards.

"Filled with treasures of merchants from many lands." This was how one writer in about 1000 described the Viking town now named York. In recent years the archeologists of the York Archeological Trust have uncovered many of these treasures. "Treasures of merchants" means that Jorvik was a rich town, made wealthy because it was the center for producing well-crafted goods that merchants traded with other parts of the Viking world and elsewhere.

How did all this come about? The Vikings had first invaded Britain in 793, when they attacked the island of Lindisfarne off the Northumbrian coast. There were more attacks from these Scandinavians. Some settled, and established villages and farms along the eastern coast of Britain. In 866 Vikings came from East Anglia and captured York, the capital of the Anglo-Saxon kingdom of Northumbria. Viking rule in York lasted for nearly ninety years. The last Viking king, Eric Bloodaxe, was expelled in 954 by the Saxons.

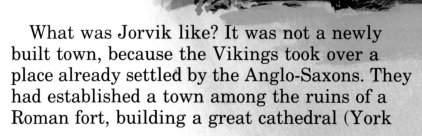

What was Jorvik like? It was not a newly built town, because the Vikings took over a place already settled by the Anglo-Saxons. They had established a town among the ruins of a Roman fort, building a great cathedral (York

Minster) inside its defensive walls. The Vikings did a lot more building as the population grew larger. One writer claimed that there were 30,000 people in the town in the tenth century.

From recent excavations, archeologists have discovered a good deal about what the people of Jorvik did and how they lived. Two types of houses were in use. The houses were twenty-three feet (about seven meters) long, and thirteen feet (over four meters) wide. They were wooden, with walls built either of wattle and daub, or made of planks of wood. Jorvik had some very skillful woodworkers. Inside, the floors were of earth, trampled flat and hard. The family lived together in one room—cooking, eating, and sleeping inside the warm, well-built house. Imagine you are one of those children in the Jorvik street—sniff the air and breathe in the smells of woodsmoke, stews, and the herbs hanging on the walls. You'd also smell the latrine behind the house!

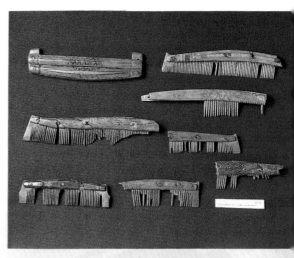

Experts working in bone and antler made thousands of combs for people to tidy their hair—and also to get out the lice and nits!

In 1958 after several years of careful exploration and recording remains in Turkey, the British archeologist James Mellaart discovered a complete town dating back to about 6500 B.C. It must have been an exciting moment when the excavations began, and almost on the first day of the dig a wall painting came to light.

Çatal Hüyük (say "*shah-tal hoo-yook*") is unique in many ways. One of the discoveries was a wall painting, showing a plan of the town with a volcano in the background. The excavations have revealed a lot about the houses of the people and the shrines to the Mother Goddess.

> FACT BOX
>
> Mud bricks were made to a uniform size—3″ × 6¼″ × 12½″ (8 × 16 × 32 centimeters)—based on the size of human hands and feet.
> Only one-thirtieth of the total area of Çatal Hüyük has been excavated so far.

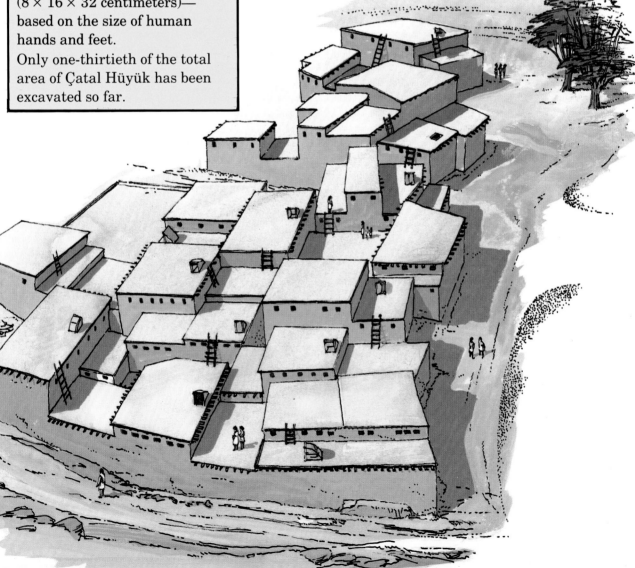

James Mellaart found a whole cluster of buildings, one attached to another like modern row houses. They were all built of wooden frames filled with mud bricks. None of the buildings had windows or doors—the only entrance was via the flat roof. You had to walk on the roof and then climb down a ladder into each building. The people of Çatal Hüyük probably built their homes like this to make them more secure against enemies.

Çatal Hüyük is one of the settlements of the early farmers in the Middle East. What did the people do? They knew how to cultivate wheat, barley, and different sorts of vegetables. They tamed and bred cattle, and also caught and used wild sheep. There was some hunting of other wild animals, but they didn't rely on this for food. Some of the people of Çatal Hüyük had useful skills. They could make clothes out of wool and animal skins, and construct all sorts of objects out of wood, bone, stone, and metal. The buildings show how good they were at working in timber and at making bricks out of sun-dried mud. The walls were covered with a daub of mud and straw, and then plastered and painted. There were about 6,000 people living in Çatal Hüyük.

This cutaway drawing is of one of the houses at Çatal Hüyük. It is very simple in plan—only one large room about nineteen feet (six meters) by thirteen feet (four meters). The room has a fireplace (the exit in the roof is just above to let out the smoke), an oven nearby against the wall, and benches along the walls. Some areas are raised up— perhaps these were sleeping areas.

This cutaway drawing shows a shrine. This is a special place where the Mother Goddess was worshiped. On the walls are skulls of bulls that have been carefully plastered and painted to look real. Also on the walls are paintings in red of vultures swooping down on headless human beings. We think the people exposed the corpses of the dead for vultures and wild animals like jackals and boars to strip off the flesh. Skeletons were buried in the shrines with the skulls left lying on top.

5 Building the Pyramid of Khufu

FACT BOX

Khufu's Great Pyramid is the biggest pyramid of all.

It is made from over 2,300,000 blocks of limestone, transported from quarries at Trura on the eastern side of the Nile.

Each block for the core weighs about twenty-seven and a half tons (about twenty-five tonnes).

The archeologist Sir Flinders Petrie found living quarters for about 4,000 specialist workers nearby, but there may have been 100,000 people employed on the site at various times.

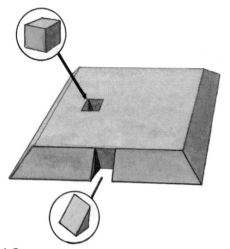

From the earliest times in Egypt, kings and other important people were buried in fine tombs. At first special buildings of mud brick, called *mastabas*, were constructed. Later these mastabas were built of stone. Some people were buried in tombs cut into rock. This type of burial place became very popular—the famous Tutankhamen was buried in one. The best known of all the Egyptian tombs are the pyramids. The first pyramids were called step pyramids because each side was constructed like a flight of stairs. The Egyptian architects and builders gradually discovered how to construct a smooth-sided pyramid, the true pyramid.

Probably the most famous of all the pyramids is the Great Pyramid at Giza, near Cairo in northern Egypt. It was built for King Khufu (also known as Cheops, the Greek form of his name). Khufu reigned from 2575 to 2550 B.C. The Great Pyramid has been surveyed many times to find out how it was built.

Stage 1

After the site was chosen (it had to be on the west side of the Nile River for religious reasons), a square was cleared of sand down to solid rock. Each side of the base of the pyramid of Khufu measured 252 yards (230 meters). The builders needed a level surface to work from, so trenches were dug and water was diverted from the Nile. As water finds its own level, it was easy to see where there were ups or downs on the site.

Stage 2

Once the site was level, the building blocks could be put into place. The builders started in the middle, and constructed a flat layer of stone blocks to form a perfect square. To make sure it was square, they used rectangular and triangular blocks. Triangular blocks were also used on the outside to make the angles of the pyramid.

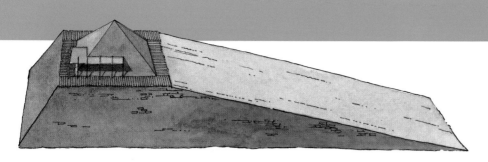

Stage 3

This process was repeated until the full height of the pyramid was reached. On top of the last layer, a pyramid-shaped capstone was fitted. The builders had gradually built an enormous ramp of earth and bricks about 5,000 feet (nearly 1,500 meters) long to get the stone to the upper levels. The ramp and the scaffolding were removed as the outside walls were cut smooth.

Inside the Pyramid

The pyramid contained the burial chambers for the king. Here you can see a cutaway section of Khufu's pyramid. During the time the pyramid was being built, King Khufu changed his mind about where he wanted to be buried— there are two abandoned chambers below the one he was buried in. The chambers, the entrance passageways, and the shafts were all constructed as the pyramid was built, not hollowed out later. When King Khufu died, his mummified body was placed in a great stone coffin in the inner chamber, and all the entrances were sealed. This did not stop tomb robbers from breaking in, though!

Pyramids at Giza today. The Great Pyramid of Khufu is the biggest.

A	vulture	J	serpent	R	mouth
B	leg	K	basket	S	cloth
D	hand	L	lion	T	loaf
F	viper	M	owl	W	chick
G	stand	N	water	Y	reeds
H	rope	P	stool	Z	bolt
I	reed	Q	hill		

The Egyptians used pictures for their writing—pictures called hieroglyphs. The pictures stood for whole words at first, but gradually came to represent sounds. The Egyptians didn't use some of the letters in our alphabet like E and O. Try writing your name, or a letter to someone, in hieroglyphs. It could be your own secret code!

Four thousand years ago, Knossos was the most important place in the land of the Keftiu. Imagine a great procession going into the palace in honor of the Snake Goddess, with the priestesses, the priests, and their helpers in the front. The priest-king is leading the first bull. It will be sacrificed to the goddess, and offerings of wine (libations) will be poured out from special jars called rhytons. One is shaped like a huge bull's head. The bull is very important here—

Fragments of many wall paintings have survived. This one shows a favorite sport—bull-leaping. At the front the girl acrobat has grabbed the bull's horns. The bull will toss her up and she will somersault across the bull's back. At the other end another acrobat stands ready to catch her. A very dangerous game!

bulls' horns were even carved in stone on the tops of the buildings. The palace is magnificent inside. There are hundreds of rooms with fine paintings on the walls. There is water running in pipes to some of the rooms—and there are baths. The palace is eerie as well as grand. There are many dark passageways. Some say it was once ruled by King Minos, who had a great beast, called the Minotaur, half man and half bull, that was given humans as a sacrifice.

Today it is possible to walk right around the great Palace of Knossos on the Greek island of Crete. Knossos was excavated beginning in the year 1900 by the great British archeologist, Sir Arthur Evans. He bought part of the site from a local landowner, and dug on an enormous scale. He also reconstructed parts of the palace and its wall paintings. He called the people who lived in Crete from around 2000 B.C. to around 1400 B.C. the Minoans, after their legendary king Minos. The Egyptians knew them as "the people of the land of Keftiu" because the Cretans brought gifts to the pharoahs, and traded with them.

Crete was heavily populated at this time and had a number of palaces, country houses, and towns. The people constructed their buildings in a special way—they had to be earthquake-proof. The walls were made of frames constructed from great wooden beams. The space in between the beams was filled with stone blocks. This helped the whole building withstand earth tremors even if part of the walls fell out. Some archeologists believe that life in the Minoan palaces came to an end around 1470 B.C. because of an enormous eruption of the volcano of Santorini, an island north of Crete.

FACT BOX

Knossos first excavated by Sir Arthur Evans. He started work in 1900. Recent excavations at Knossos have produced evidence of human sacrifice.

Knossos is near Herakleion in Crete.

While excavating at the Minoan town of Akrotiri on Santorini in 1967, the Greek archeologist Spyridon Marinatos found evidence of an enormous eruption of the island's volcano.

The Minoans were great traders, sailing all over the eastern Mediterranean Sea.

The Throne Room at Knossos has reconstructed walls and ceiling. The wall paintings, also reconstructed, are from fragments found in the excavations. It is easy to see why Sir Arthur Evans called this the Throne Room. However, it is more likely to have been the special room of a Minoan priestess.

Imagine you are living in the Roman world. Perhaps you are in the countryside sitting in the shade of the great arches of an aqueduct, with the water swooshing along in the stone channels high above you. Perhaps the peace of the warm afternoon is broken by the tramp of soldiers' hobnailed sandals on some stone road in the distance. Perhaps you are imagining yourself in a great town or city bustling with life. This is what the Roman writer Juvenal said: "However fast we hurry there's a huge crowd ahead and the mob behind is pushing and shoving. You get dug in the ribs by someone's elbow. The streets are filthy—our legs are plastered with mud, someone tramples your feet or a soldier's hobnailed sandal lands right on your toe. Togas which have only just been patched are torn."

Just along the bay from the great Roman city of Neapolis—the New City—now called Naples—were several towns. Two of them have become very famous because they were rediscovered and have been excavated. The Romans called these towns Pompeii and Herculaneum.

These towns were doing well in the first century A.D. They were full of rich merchants and shopkeepers who were proud to live there. They wanted their town to be as fine as Rome itself—the capital city of the Roman Empire. In Pompeii there were large open squares, a great town hall, several public baths, a theater which could hold 5,000 people, and an amphitheater where 20,000 could watch animals and people being torn apart and killed.

The town had an old center (like many of our towns today) but new areas had been added. There were a number of long, straight streets crammed with shops that spilled out onto the pavements. Here you might have to walk around someone making something—carving a chair leg, for example—or people filling the pavement at one of the public water fountains. In the picture is a baker's shop, called in Latin (the Romans' language) a *pistrinum*. It's more than a shop—there the owners can say not only that they bake fresh on the premises but also that the flour is freshly ground.

Disaster strikes

You would have been very unlucky to have
visited Pompeii or Herculaneum on August 24,
in the year 79. On this day the nearby volcano,
Vesuvius, erupted, hurling ash and stones
many miles around. Debris nearly 13 feet
(4 meters) deep covered Pompeii, and
Herculaneum was swallowed up in liquid mud.
Thousands died of suffocation or were buried by
falling buildings. The towns were lost. Vesuvius
erupted ten more times after that.

*The archeologist Giuseppe Fiorelli
poured liquid plaster into holes he
discovered in the hardened ash and
stones at Pompeii. When the plaster
set, he was able to excavate the
shapes of people and animals that
had rotted away.*

The towns rediscovered

The towns of Pompeii and Herculaneum were
rediscovered, quite by accident, in 1594.
Excavations did not start until 1748, but they
were not like the careful work of archeologists
today. Although large areas were opened up,
the work was really little more than treasure
hunting. The first careful excavations began in
1860 when Giuseppe Fiorelli was appointed
Director of Excavations. He made records of his
work, and conserved the buildings he uncovered.

*This picture, by Francesco
Piranesi.shows the eruption of
Vesuvius on August 8, 1779.*

AUGINE

CAVE CAN EM

26

A Family Home in Pompeii

We are standing in the street just outside this house. Hey, watch out! The street is very crowded today—it's market day and many of the traders are out selling their goods to the passersby. Here's the front door of the house, between two shops. If you peer in through the iron grille you can see the sort of welcome strangers can expect—*cave canem*—beware the dog! It's quite likely there is no dog at this house, but there will be a doorman who acts as a watchdog to keep us out unless we are friends of the family or have a business appointment with the owner. He's a wine merchant who buys from the vineyards on the slopes of Vesuvius and sells in his shop at the front of his house.

He's well off. Look at the way the hall is decorated. The hall, called an *atrium*, has a stone-and-mosaic floor with a pool, the *impluvium*, to catch the rainwater from the skylight above. It looks good and provides water for the kitchen.

Look past the children in the hall into the room with its shutters open. This is where the master of the house does the accounts for his wine business. That is the main living room of the house, called the *tablinum*. He has the shutters open on the other side of the room, so we can see into the garden. There is a shady walk under a roof supported by columns. In the far corner you can just glimpse the family shrine. That is where little offerings of cakes with honey and wine are made to the special gods and goddesses who look after this family.

In the tablinum of this house in Pompeii a fine mosaic was found. It shows a behind-the-scenes rehearsal for a play. Can you see the actors' masks? One actor on the left is being dressed for a part, and the musician is playing an instrument called the double pipes.

Only the most important people of the city are allowed in here. It's the Great Bath, where the ritual or ceremonial cleansing takes place before the gods and goddesses are worshiped. The bath is deep enough to plunge your whole body in—head as well. Around the outside of the courtyard is a walkway, shaded from the burning sun by its overhanging roof. Beyond that are the changing rooms—some with their own little baths.

FACT BOX

The city, near the River Indus in Sind, was discovered by R. D. Banerjii of the Archeological Survey of India in 1922. Excavations began the same year.

Mohenjo-Daro stands today in hot, dry countryside, but the climate has changed in the four thousand years since it was built.

Mohenjo-Daro, in Pakistan, is the name we give to the largest city of the Indus civilization, developed along the valley of the Indus River. It was an area rich in wildlife and, with rainfall higher in the past than now, good for growing crops.

This city was established around 2500 B.C. and the evidence from archeological surveys and excavations shows that the people were very well organized. The city of Mohenjo-Daro had a population of about 4,000 and was constructed on two large mounds.

The smaller mound had public buildings on it, including the Great Bath. There was also a huge storehouse raised off the ground so that air could circulate and keep the precious harvest dry. A great square building, eighty feet (twenty-four meters) square with its roof supported by pillars, is thought to have been a meeting hall. What does this evidence suggest? Some of the men of Mohenjo-Daro were rulers— perhaps also priests. They had special buildings for ceremonies (like the Great Bath and hall). They stored the produce of the community in a nearby granary. Perhaps they handed it out to those who lived and worked in the lower city.

The much larger mound contained the lower city. This had been carefully planned into large rectangular blocks with streets nearly thirty feet (nine meters) wide. Inside each block were houses, shops, and some temples. The houses varied enormously in their size, from two rooms to mansions with two or three inner courtyards.

The people of the Indus Valley were farmers who kept a variety of animals like cattle, sheep, pigs, dogs, and buffaloes. They probably also used horses, elephants, and camels. They grew wheat, barley, vegetables, and sometimes rice. The inhabitants of Mohenjo-Daro were probably not farmers, but exchanged their trades, skills, and labor for food doled out by the officials in the higher city. There were shopkeepers, potters, dyers, sculptors, jewelry makers, and metal workers. There were also dancing girls, garbage collectors, and sewage workers.

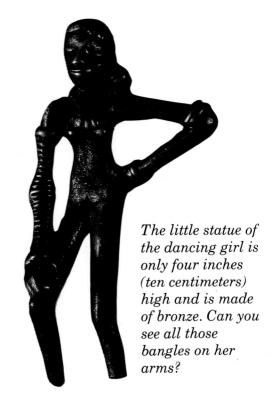

The little statue of the dancing girl is only four inches (ten centimeters) high and is made of bronze. Can you see all those bangles on her arms?

One of the many seals found in the city. The original was cut in stone and used to make an impression on clay attached to a merchant's bale or box of goods. Archeologists have not been able to decipher the script — perhaps it's the name of the merchant.

One of the straight streets at Mohenjo-Daro. The street itself is not paved but has a drain, or sewer, running down one side. The channel is covered with stone, and there are manholes for cleaning it out or repairing it. The waste from the bathrooms and lavatories of the private houses and workshops was taken away in a very elaborate system of underground channels running under the building throughout the city. The houses had garbage chutes through the walls to brick boxes on the outside walls—to be emptied by garbage collectors.

9 The Stone Walls of Great Zimbabwe

From the air the site of Great Zimbabwe can be seen to be circular.

It is 1871. A man with a huge beard is approaching, crushing the undergrowth with his great hobnailed boots. He wears a leather hat, and a suit made out of antelope skin. He is carrying an umbrella, various weapons, a blanket, bags, and many boxes. He is Karl Mauch, a German geologist and explorer who has reached the end of a long trail to find the ruins associated with the famous ruler of the Shona people, Mutota.

Karl Mauch did indeed reach those ruins, in the country then known as Mashonaland. This later became Rhodesia, and it is now called Zimbabwe. Karl Mauch found it difficult to investigate the ruins he had found because they were so overgrown, but he did publish a book about his discoveries when he reached home. He thought that these extraordinary stone buildings were the gold mines of King Solomon, the biblical king of Israel. People believed this incorrect idea for many years.

Eventually archeologists began to investigate this mysterious place. By the 1920s archeologists were sure that Great Zimbabwe, as the site was called, was built by African peoples in the medieval period.

By the 1970s much excavation and investigation, at Great Zimbabwe and elsewhere, had taken place. The history of the site is now clear.

The hill at Great Zimbabwe was occupied first in the second to fourth centuries A.D., by farming peoples who spoke the Bantu language. These inhabitants could make tools and weapons out of iron. By the eleventh century the ancestors of the present Shona people had built a settlement there. It became an important center for gold working and trade. Great Zimbabwe's most impressive stone buildings were constructed in the fourteenth and fifteenth centuries, when the population was over 3,000 people, mainly cattle farmers. In this capital city, luxury items such as beads from Malaya and India and porcelain from China have been excavated—evidence that the citizens traded their gold far across the world. The leaders or chiefs at Great Zimbabwe probably controlled a large territory around the town.

Much of the ruins survive today. They look like walls to defend the site—and there are even tall towers in places. Archeologists now think that this stone construction was mainly for show. Around the stone buildings would have been a large number of wood and mud houses for the people of Great Zimbabwe.

The gentle slopes of the hill do not look as though there is anything special underneath them!

Although you may have never heard the name Ch'in Shi-huang-ti, you've probably seen pictures of his most famous construction—the Great Wall of China. When this emperor came to power in 221 B.C. he began to bring the vast country together into a single empire. His own family, or dynasty, ruled for only eleven years, but the systems he set up for government lasted until 1912. He protected the great empire with a solid wall from the invasions of barbarians outside to the north. Throughout the empire people used laws, money, weights and measures and writing—all of which he standardized.

A most fantastic discovery was made at Mount Li in China in March 1974 by farmers digging wells for water. They accidentally stumbled upon a series of huge pits containing about 7,000 clay warriors! This was the site of the tomb or burial place of China's first emperor, Ch'in Shi-huang-ti.

FACT BOX

The pottery warriors were first discovered in 1974, by farmers digging a well at Mount Li in Shansi province in northern China.

Every single one of Ch'in Shi-huang-ti's pottery warriors has a different face.

The Emperor Ch'in Shi-huang-ti founded the Ch'in Dynasty, and reigned from 221 to 210 B.C.

Rank upon rank of soldiers, as they would have been formed up to go to war. Are the statues portraits of the men of Ch'in Shi-huang-ti's army?

An archer kneels in readiness.

A great army of clay warriors! Excavation of one of the burial pits at Mount Li is under way. A huge cover has been placed over the excavations to allow the site to be protected and be seen by visitors.

The emperor was buried a mile (one and a half kilometers) away under a huge mound of earth 4,500 feet (1,400 meters) square. Close around the mound was a wall with four gates. Around that was a great courtyard measuring about 6,600 by 3,300 feet (2,000 by 1,000 meters). Inside this courtyard was a building for servants, guards, and attendants. By the time of the first emperor, the Chinese were no longer burying live guards and attendants with rulers and kings. Statues of them, made from pottery and bronze were buried inside to protect and serve the emperor in the afterlife.

This was just what those lucky farmers, and later the archeologists, found—but on a grand scale! Three pits were discovered. The biggest, now called Pit Number 1, measures about 690 by 195 feet (210 by 60 meters). The life-size figures are in battle formation, standing in a number of corridors—each one paved, and with a strong roof. In this pit were over 3,000 foot soldiers as well as bowmen, spearmen, and officers, all with their weapons, and six chariots —complete with pottery horses.

The whole pit was covered with woven matting and a thick layer of clay. Although the other two pits had been broken into at the end of the Ch'in dynasty, Pit Number 1 survived intact—a secret city of the dead to be discovered over 2,100 years later.

An officer from a horse-drawn chariot.

Cleaning the statues is a delicate task.

"These structures are very well preserved, though they have been abandoned by their inhabitants for several centuries. Among the fine, dry dust or the fallen blocks of sandstone that have filled the rooms, we still find in a wonderful state of preservation the household articles and implements once used by the inhabitants of the cliff-dwellings"—wrote Gustav Nordenskjöld, an archeologist working at Mesa Verde in 1891.

The ruins that Gustav Nordenskjöld described are at Mesa Verde in Colorado in the southwestern United States. They were first discovered in 1874 when this area was explored by the United States Geological and Geographical Survey. Later investigations and excavations revealed a number of settlements of the Anasazi Indians, who lived here between 350 and 1300.

Archeologists often use the word *pueblo* to describe this period. The word itself means "village." The earliest people came to the mesas (high, long ridges) and the canyons about 100 B.C. and they built villages on the mesas. Later, around 1100, the Anasazi Indians began to build dwellings under the overhanging ledges of the cliffs.

They used the local sandstone, as well as wood and mortar made of mud, to build their settlements. They needed as much of the precious space as possible, so they built apartment blocks to live in—some were four stories high. Even though they were already well protected by their position under the cliff, which was difficult and dangerous to get to, they also built watch towers. They wanted to be secure from their enemies, the Athapaskan Indians, as well as wild animals. Besides their living quarters, there were a number of special rooms called *kivas*. These were circular, and used as community meeting places for religious and other ceremonies. A hole cut in the floor, called a *sipapu*, was thought to be the entrance to the spirit world that was below the ground. The people were farmers, cultivating crops like corn, squash, and beans. They bred turkeys, and also hunted and collected a great variety of food—fruit, eggs, squirrel, rats, and deer.

The Anasazi Indians were excellent potters, making hundreds of bowls, jars, and mugs out of clay that they fired. The black and white patterns used as decoration on the pots are simple, but very striking.

12 Machu Picchu The Lost City of the Incas

"Suddenly we found ourselves in the midst of a jungle-covered maze of small and large walls, the ruins of buildings made of white granite, most carefully cut and fitted together without cement. Surprise followed surprise until there came the realization that we were in the midst of as wonderful ruins as ever found in Peru"— wrote Hiram Bingham, who discovered Machu Picchu in 1911.

The year after Hiram Bingham discovered Machu Picchu he began excavating there, leading an expedition from Yale University in the United States. This small town of the Incas in the Andes Mountains of Peru has now been completely uncovered.

Who were the Incas? They were originally a powerful family who first controlled a small, mountainous area. Gradually they built an empire that stretched along the east coast of South America into the present-day countries of Ecuador, Peru, Bolivia, Chile, and Argentina. Their leader was known as *Sapa Inca*, which means "the only emperor." The emperor ruled from the capital city, Cuzco, not far from the town of Machu Picchu.

The first powerful Inca family, led by Manco Capac, arrived in Cuzco about 1100. Machu Picchu was built sometime after 1438, in the reign of Pachacuti Inca Yupanqui. The Incas turned a landscape of mountains, jungles, and desert coasts into a rich country. They were excellent engineers, building over 14,300 miles (23,000 kilometers) of paved roads throughout the empire. This great civilization came to an end when the Inca people were conquered by the Spanish, who invaded in 1532.

The Incas did not have writing but did keep records. Records and accounts of goods brought into the town's storehouses were very important in such an organized empire. The Quipucamayoc were special accountants appointed to do just that. They used the quipu *to keep accounts. It is a cord from which hang a series of colored strings with knots tied in them. We cannot work out exactly what it says but we do know that the Incas counted in tens. A sort of* quipu *is still used today by herdsmen in the Andes Mountains.*

Inca builders and farmers were very good at getting the best out of the mountainous country.

They built terraces, creating long narrow fields kept in by stone walls. At different levels on the mountain slopes they grew maize cobs, beans, and potatoes. Occasionally they ate guinea pigs. They also kept flocks of llamas (mainly to carry goods) and alpacas (for their wool). The Inca people paid taxes in the form of about two-thirds of the crops they produced. This food was stored in each town ready to give out to the sick, the old, or anyone in need.

The picture opposite shows the magnificent festival called Capac Raymi. In Cuzco the Sapa Inca is leading his people in worship of Inti, the Sun God. Here in Machu Picchu a member of the Inca royal family and the priests are leading a procession to the Temple of the Sun. The Incas believed that their gods controlled the world around them—occasionally it was necessary to make sacrifices to a particular god.

The town of Machu Picchu was built for about 1,000 people and covers about 100 acres (40 hectares) of land. It is defended by sheer drops on three sides and on the fourth by a dry moat and defensive walls of stone. Like other Inca towns it was carefully planned. Various buildings (storehouses, palace, prison, temple, and houses) surround a great plaza or public square. There were also burial places—special tombs hollowed out of the rock.

The Incas were skillful builders. They cut granite, a very hard rock, with stone hammers. They used irregular blocks for their houses and rectangular shapes for doorways, windows, and for very important buildings. They loved the trapezoidal shape of the windows and doorways, which gave them spectacular views of the mountains around.

Their houses were quite simple. A family lived in a one-room house. They slept on mats on the floor. There was no furniture except stone benches along the wall. Houses were often grouped together as large family units around a courtyard.

It's a warm spring day in 1771—the St. George's Day Fair on April 23. Folk from all around have gathered with the townspeople of Williamsburg to buy and sell their wares and enjoy themselves. In the background of Market Square is the new courthouse, built only last year. It's a fine brick building with a tower and large pediment (the triangular structure over the front door), looking like part of an ancient Greek temple.

A great fair is held here twice a year. The other one is on December 12, but today's is better. People are happier now—they know that winter is over and the warm summer is coming. Farmers bring their livestock to sell and trade, merchants carry goods from all over the territory of Virginia to set up their stalls for the day. There are games and entertainment everywhere. There are contests, too—contests for the beauty queen, for dancing, and playing the fiddle. The most exciting is the pig chase—

people try to catch a pig by its tail. That's not as easy as it looks—you try grabbing a pig's little tail with soap all over it!

In 1585 the British established their first colony in America. Sir Walter Raleigh named the new territory Virginia after the virgin, or unmarried, Queen Elizabeth I. The town of Williamsburg in Virginia was originally called Middle Plantation when it was founded by British settlers in 1633. It was a simple settlement then—an outpost of the nearby village of Jamestown, stockaded against Indian attack. By 1699, Middle Plantation had grown to a small village with houses, shops, and two mills. The settlement also had a college of higher education—the College of William and Mary. According to an early account this college was "first modelled by Sir Christopher Wren," the British architect of St. Paul's Cathedral in London.

In 1699, Middle Plantation became the capital of Virginia, and was renamed Williamsburg in honor of King William III. As the town grew, all sorts of private and public buildings were put up: public buildings like the Capitol, where the assembly of Virginia discussed and passed laws. There was also the town's public jail, the parish church, a powder magazine and guardhouse, and America's first theater, built about 1716. The town grew according to a careful plan. It was based on two streets that crossed at right angles. The main street was called Duke of Gloucester Street. Other streets were laid out on a grid, rather like a Roman town or Mohenjo-Daro, forming square or rectangular areas for the buildings.

This is the governor's palace, the official house and offices of the seven governors appointed by the British from 1709 to 1781. Virginia was the largest of the British colonies in America and the king's representative needed an impressive residence. It stands in fine grounds, with a long lake, a bowling green, and various types of gardens.

Most ordinary houses were made of wood. These houses—frame houses—are made from a number of wall frames of wood with beams jointed together. Over that on the outside are planks of wood painted white. Usually the only brick construction in a house like this is the chimney at one or both ends of the building.

Historical Archeology

How do we know so much about Williamsburg and the buildings there? Part of the answer is that there are records and documents that have survived from the eighteenth century—things that people wrote down.

In 1901 the rector of the parish church of Williamsburg, William Archer Rutherford Goodwin, restored his own church, which was built in 1715. The Reverend Goodwin wanted to go on to restore the entire colonial capital as well. Luckily for him, and for us today, the millionaire John D. Rockefeller, Jr., visited Williamsburg in 1926 and put enormous sums of money into the project. It was decided to excavate for remains of buildings and find out from documents what these buildings had originally looked like. Now many buildings have either been restored—where some parts were still standing and needed repair—or reconstructed—rebuilt completely from plans or other documents and the evidence of pictures.

Williamsburg is still lived in today but can be visited. Many of the buildings are open to the public. For example, you can buy medicines from an apothecary's shop, or watch a gunsmith at work in a shop reconstructed from an original building of 1768. Williamsburg is now part of a protected area, the Colonial National Historical Park.

14 The Empire State Building

How many stories, or floors, does your house have? Can you look down from your bedroom window onto the yard or street outside? Perhaps you live on a street of tall apartments and your building seems to scrape the sky. Can you imagine a building 1,454 feet (over 400 meters) high with 102 floors? If you lived in New York in the 1920s you would be getting used to such tall buildings, called skyscrapers.

This view of New York City shows the Empire State Building in the foreground. The building started with a riveted steel frame. This frame is really the building's skeleton. The "flesh" of the Empire State Building is its outer skin, concrete floors, and inside walls. The exterior is mainly built of Indiana limestone and granite and trimmed with stainless steel.

45

There were various reasons why people decided to put up such tall buildings. Land in New York City was (and still is) very expensive —and many people wanted to have their offices, houses, and apartments there. Architects and builders were discovering new ways of putting up such giants. Underneath the city is a thick layer of solid rock so that the foundations of skyscrapers do not move.

In 1929 a group of business people got together a plan to put up the biggest building that New York, and the world, had ever seen. They employed the firm of Shreeve, Lamb and Harmon Associates as architects. The building was completed in 1931, and is an internationally famous landmark.

Think for Yourself

Suppose you were an archeologist of the future. What ideas would you have about the Empire State Building?

If only part of it survived (like the houses at Skara Brae) could you work out what the whole building was like? Suppose only the foundations were left—holes in the ground with the remains of concrete and steel? Could you work out the size and shape of the building? Archeologists often have to do just that, using only the holes left by posts where wooden houses once stood.

Imagine that you have collected all the possible clues about the building itself, and have a pretty good idea of what it looked like. What was it used for? is the next question. Was it a public or a private building? Did people live in it or work in it or hold special ceremonies?

Now that you have had some practice in being an archeological detective, go out and look for clues that show what your neighborhood was like in the past. You might be lucky and find one of those as yet undiscovered buildings.

Glossary

Alpaca Kind of llama with long woolly coat

Amphitheater A circular or oval building with rows of seats rising around a central open space, often used for staging games and spectacles

Amphora Greek word, taken into Latin, for a two-handled jar

Aqueduct A specially built channel for water, often carried overhead on arches

Atrium Central hall or court of Roman house

Barbarian Wild or uncultured person, usually a foreigner

Bitumen A black sticky pitch, naturally occurring form of petroleum

Canyon A deep gorge in rocky country, often with a stream at the bottom

Capac Raymi The festival of the Sun God in the Inca empire

Ch'in Dynasty The dynasty under which China first united into an empire, 221–206 B.C.

Daub Mud and straw mixture plastered onto wattles to give a smooth surface

Dynasty Succession of rulers, each inheriting power from predecessor

Frieze A band of decoration on a wall, usually near the ceiling

Granite A very hard, durable rock

Impluvium A basin in the floor of the atrium for catching rain water from the roof

Iron Age A period of history when people used tools and weapons made of iron

Kiva A circular room used for religious and other ceremonial meetings

Libations An offering of wine poured out to a god or goddess

Llama Woolly cud-chewing South American animal, used as beast of burden and related to the camel

Mastaba A tomb of brick or stone, used in ancient Egypt before pyramids were built

Mesas High, long ridges of rock with flat tops

Mosaic Way of making pictures or patterns by using small pieces of stone, glass, or other hard-wearing materials

Minotaur A monster, half man and half bull, supposed in legend to have lived in the labyrinth of King Minos

Mortaria High-sided bowl used for grinding up herbs and spices—mortar

Neolithic A time before written history, when people used tools and weapons made of stone

Pediment Triangular structure over portico or porch of building designed in the style of classical Greece

Pistrinium The Latin word for a baker's shop

Plaza A Spanish word for a market place or open square

Pueblo Town or village in Latin America

Quipu An arrangement of cords used by the Incas for counting

Quipucamayoc The accountants of the Inca empire

Radiocarbon dating A method of dating ancient organic material by measuring the radioactivity of carbon

Rhyton A special jar, often highly decorated, used to hold wine and other offerings made to a shrine or temple

Sapa Inca "The only Inca"—the ruler of the Inca empire

Shrines Altars dedicated to a god or goddess

Sipapu A hole cut in the floor of a kiva, thought to be the entrance to the underground spirit world

Tablinum The living room of a Roman house

Thermopolium The Latin word for a shop where hot food could be bought and taken away

Toga The loose outer clothing of a Roman citizen

Trapezoidal A four-sided shape with no two sides parallel

Wattle Branches and sticks woven together to make fences, walls, and roofs

Index